ADDRESS BOOK
KITTY

The Pocket Size Address Book

www.journalsrus.com

Address Book Kitty
© 2016 Ciparum LLC
ISBN-10:1-63589-058-6
ISBN-13:978-1-63589-058-7

Table of Content

Name	Page		Name	Page

Name	Page		Name	Page

THIS PAGE WAS
INTENTIONALLY
LEFT BLANK

NAME...

ADDRESS...

....

MOBILE # (Cell)..

HOME #...

WORK #...

FAX..

EMAIL...

NAME...

ADDRESS...

....

MOBILE # (Cell)..

HOME #...

WORK #...

FAX..

EMAIL...

NAME...

ADDRESS...

....

MOBILE # (Cell)..

HOME #...

WORK #...

FAX..

EMAIL...

NOTES:

NAME..

ADDRESS..

....

MOBILE # (Cell)..

HOME #...

WORK #...

FAX...

EMAIL..

NAME..

ADDRESS..

....

MOBILE # (Cell)..

HOME #...

WORK #...

FAX...

EMAIL..

NAME..

ADDRESS..

....

MOBILE # (Cell)..

HOME #...

WORK #...

FAX...

EMAIL..

NOTES:

NAME..

ADDRESS..

....

MOBILE # (Cell)...

HOME #...

WORK #...

FAX..

EMAIL...

NAME..

ADDRESS..

....

MOBILE # (Cell)...

HOME #...

WORK #...

FAX..

EMAIL...

NAME..

ADDRESS..

....

MOBILE # (Cell)...

HOME #...

WORK #...

FAX..

EMAIL...

NOTES:

NAME..

ADDRESS..

....

MOBILE # (Cell)..

HOME #..

WORK #..

FAX..

EMAIL..

NAME..

ADDRESS..

....

MOBILE # (Cell)..

HOME #..

WORK #..

FAX..

EMAIL..

NAME..

ADDRESS..

....

MOBILE # (Cell)..

HOME #..

WORK #..

FAX..

EMAIL..

NOTES:

4

NAME..

ADDRESS...

....

MOBILE # (Cell)...

HOME #...

WORK #...

FAX..

EMAIL...

NAME..

ADDRESS...

....

MOBILE # (Cell)...

HOME #...

WORK #...

FAX..

EMAIL...

NAME..

ADDRESS...

....

MOBILE # (Cell)...

HOME #...

WORK #...

FAX..

EMAIL...

NOTES:

NAME..

ADDRESS..

....

MOBILE # (Cell)..

HOME #...

WORK #..

FAX..

EMAIL...

NAME..

ADDRESS..

....

MOBILE # (Cell)..

HOME #...

WORK #..

FAX..

EMAIL...

NAME..

ADDRESS..

....

MOBILE # (Cell)..

HOME #...

WORK #..

FAX..

EMAIL...

NOTES:

NAME...
ADDRESS...
....
MOBILE # (Cell)..
HOME #...
WORK #...
FAX..
EMAIL..

NAME...
ADDRESS...
....
MOBILE # (Cell)..
HOME #...
WORK #...
FAX..
EMAIL..

NAME...
ADDRESS...
....
MOBILE # (Cell)..
HOME #...
WORK #...
FAX..
EMAIL..

NOTES:

NAME...
ADDRESS..
....
MOBILE # (Cell)...
HOME #...
WORK #...
FAX..
EMAIL...

NAME...
ADDRESS..
....
MOBILE # (Cell)...
HOME #...
WORK #...
FAX..
EMAIL...

NAME...
ADDRESS..
....
MOBILE # (Cell)...
HOME #...
WORK #...
FAX..
EMAIL...

NOTES:

NAME..

ADDRESS..

....

MOBILE # (Cell)..

HOME #...

WORK #...

FAX...

EMAIL..

NAME..

ADDRESS..

....

MOBILE # (Cell)..

HOME #...

WORK #...

FAX ....

EMAIL..

NAME..

ADDRESS..

....

MOBILE # (Cell)..

HOME #...

WORK #...

FAX...

EMAIL..

NOTES:

NAME..

ADDRESS...

....

MOBILE # (Cell)...

HOME #..

WORK #..

FAX...

EMAIL..

NAME..

ADDRESS...

....

MOBILE # (Cell)...

HOME #..

WORK #..

FAX...

EMAIL..

NAME..

ADDRESS...

....

MOBILE # (Cell)...

HOME #..

WORK #..

FAX...

EMAIL..

NOTES:

NAME..

ADDRESS...

....

MOBILE # (Cell)...

HOME #..

WORK #..

FAX...

EMAIL..

NAME..

ADDRESS...

....

MOBILE # (Cell)...

HOME #..

WORK #..

FAX...

EMAIL..

NAME..

ADDRESS...

....

MOBILE # (Cell)...

HOME #..

WORK #..

FAX...

EMAIL..

NOTES:

NAME..

ADDRESS..

....

MOBILE # (Cell)...

HOME #..

WORK #..

FAX..

EMAIL..

NAME..

ADDRESS..

....

MOBILE # (Cell)...

HOME #..

WORK #..

FAX..

EMAIL..

NAME..

ADDRESS..

....

MOBILE # (Cell)...

HOME #..

WORK #..

FAX..

EMAIL..

NOTES:

NAME...
ADDRESS...
....
MOBILE # (Cell)..
HOME #...
WORK #..
FAX...
EMAIL..

NAME...
ADDRESS...
....
MOBILE # (Cell)..
HOME #...
WORK #..
FAX...
EMAIL..

NAME...
ADDRESS...
....
MOBILE # (Cell)..
HOME #...
WORK #..
FAX...
EMAIL..

NOTES:

NAME..

ADDRESS...

....

MOBILE # (Cell)...

HOME #...

WORK #...

FAX..

EMAIL..

NAME..

ADDRESS...

....

MOBILE # (Cell)...

HOME #...

WORK #...

FAX..

EMAIL..

NAME..

ADDRESS...

....

MOBILE # (Cell)...

HOME #...

WORK #...

FAX..

EMAIL..

NOTES:

NAME..

ADDRESS...

....

MOBILE # (Cell)..

HOME #..

WORK #..

FAX...

EMAIL..

NAME..

ADDRESS...

....

MOBILE # (Cell)..

HOME #..

WORK #..

FAX...

EMAIL..

NAME..

ADDRESS...

....

MOBILE # (Cell)..

HOME #..

WORK #..

FAX...

EMAIL..

NOTES:

NAME...

ADDRESS..

....

MOBILE # (Cell)..

HOME #...

WORK #..

FAX...

EMAIL..

NAME...

ADDRESS..

....

MOBILE # (Cell)..

HOME #...

WORK #..

FAX...

EMAIL..

NAME...

ADDRESS..

....

MOBILE # (Cell)..

HOME #...

WORK #..

FAX...

EMAIL..

NOTES:

NAME...

ADDRESS..

....

MOBILE # (Cell)...

HOME #..

WORK #..

FAX..

EMAIL..

NAME...

ADDRESS..

....

MOBILE # (Cell)...

HOME #..

WORK #..

FAX..

EMAIL..

NAME...

ADDRESS..

....

MOBILE # (Cell)...

HOME #..

WORK #..

FAX..

EMAIL..

NOTES:

NAME..

ADDRESS..

....

MOBILE # (Cell)..

HOME #...

WORK #..

FAX...

EMAIL...

NAME..

ADDRESS..

....

MOBILE # (Cell)..

HOME #...

WORK #..

FAX...

EMAIL...

NAME..

ADDRESS..

....

MOBILE # (Cell)..

HOME #...

WORK #..

FAX...

EMAIL...

NOTES:

NAME..

ADDRESS...

....

MOBILE # (Cell)..

HOME #..

WORK #..

FAX...

EMAIL..

NAME..

ADDRESS...

....

MOBILE # (Cell)..

HOME #..

WORK #..

FAX...

EMAIL..

NAME..

ADDRESS...

....

MOBILE # (Cell)..

HOME #..

WORK #..

FAX...

EMAIL..

NOTES:

NAME..

ADDRESS...

....

MOBILE # (Cell)...

HOME #..

WORK #..

FAX...

EMAIL..

NAME..

ADDRESS...

....

MOBILE # (Cell)...

HOME #..

WORK #..

FAX...

EMAIL..

NAME..

ADDRESS...

....

MOBILE # (Cell)...

HOME #..

WORK #..

FAX...

EMAIL..

NOTES:

NAME...

ADDRESS...

....

MOBILE # (Cell)...

HOME #...

WORK #...

FAX...

EMAIL..

NAME...

ADDRESS...

....

MOBILE # (Cell)...

HOME #...

WORK #...

FAX...

EMAIL..

NAME...

ADDRESS...

....

MOBILE # (Cell)...

HOME #...

WORK #...

FAX...

EMAIL..

NOTES:

NAME...

ADDRESS..

....

MOBILE # (Cell)..

HOME #..

WORK #...

FAX..

EMAIL..

NAME...

ADDRESS..

....

MOBILE # (Cell)..

HOME #..

WORK #...

FAX..

EMAIL..

NAME...

ADDRESS..

....

MOBILE # (Cell)..

HOME #..

WORK #...

FAX..

EMAIL..

NOTES:

NAME..
ADDRESS...
....
MOBILE # (Cell)..
HOME #..
WORK #..
FAX...
EMAIL..

NAME..
ADDRESS...
....
MOBILE # (Cell)..
HOME #..
WORK #..
FAX...
EMAIL..

NAME..
ADDRESS...
....
MOBILE # (Cell)..
HOME #..
WORK #..
FAX...
EMAIL..

NOTES:

NAME..

ADDRESS...

....

MOBILE # (Cell)..

HOME #...

WORK #...

FAX..

EMAIL...

NAME..

ADDRESS...

....

MOBILE # (Cell)..

HOME #...

WORK #...

FAX..

EMAIL...

NAME..

ADDRESS...

....

MOBILE # (Cell)..

HOME #...

WORK #...

FAX..

EMAIL...

NOTES:

NAME..

ADDRESS..

....

MOBILE # (Cell)..

HOME #...

WORK #...

FAX...

EMAIL..

NAME..

ADDRESS..

....

MOBILE # (Cell)..

HOME #...

WORK #...

FAX...

EMAIL..

NAME..

ADDRESS..

....

MOBILE # (Cell)..

HOME #...

WORK #...

FAX...

EMAIL..

NOTES:

NAME..
ADDRESS...
....
MOBILE # (Cell)...
HOME #..
WORK #...
FAX..
EMAIL...

NAME..
ADDRESS...
....
MOBILE # (Cell)...
HOME #..
WORK #...
FAX..
EMAIL...

NAME..
ADDRESS...
....
MOBILE # (Cell)...
HOME #..
WORK #...
FAX..
EMAIL...

NOTES:

NAME..

ADDRESS...

....

MOBILE # (Cell)...

HOME #..

WORK #...

FAX..

EMAIL..

NAME..

ADDRESS...

....

MOBILE # (Cell)...

HOME #..

WORK #...

FAX..

EMAIL..

NAME..

ADDRESS...

....

MOBILE # (Cell)...

HOME #..

WORK #...

FAX..

EMAIL..

NOTES:

NAME...

ADDRESS...

....

MOBILE # (Cell)...

HOME #...

WORK #...

FAX...

EMAIL...

NAME...

ADDRESS...

....

MOBILE # (Cell)...

HOME #...

WORK #...

FAX...

EMAIL...

NAME...

ADDRESS...

....

MOBILE # (Cell)...

HOME #...

WORK #...

FAX...

EMAIL...

NOTES:

NAME..
ADDRESS...
....
MOBILE # (Cell)..
HOME #...
WORK #...
FAX..
EMAIL..

NAME..
ADDRESS...
....
MOBILE # (Cell)..
HOME #...
WORK #...
FAX..
EMAIL..

NAME..
ADDRESS...
....
MOBILE # (Cell)..
HOME #...
WORK #...
FAX..
EMAIL..

NOTES:

NAME...

ADDRESS..

....

MOBILE # (Cell)...

HOME #..

WORK #..

FAX...

EMAIL..

NAME...

ADDRESS..

....

MOBILE # (Cell)...

HOME #..

WORK #..

FAX...

EMAIL..

NAME...

ADDRESS..

....

MOBILE # (Cell)...

HOME #..

WORK #..

FAX...

EMAIL..

NOTES:

NAME..
ADDRESS..
....
MOBILE # (Cell)..
HOME #..
WORK #..
FAX..
EMAIL..

NAME..
ADDRESS..
....
MOBILE # (Cell)..
HOME #..
WORK #..
FAX..
EMAIL..

NAME..
ADDRESS..
....
MOBILE # (Cell)..
HOME #..
WORK #..
FAX..
EMAIL..

NOTES:

NAME..

ADDRESS...

....

MOBILE # (Cell)...

HOME #...

WORK #...

FAX..

EMAIL..

NAME..

ADDRESS...

....

MOBILE # (Cell)...

HOME #...

WORK #...

FAX..

EMAIL..

NAME..

ADDRESS...

....

MOBILE # (Cell)...

HOME #...

WORK #...

FAX..

EMAIL..

NOTES:

NAME...

ADDRESS..

....

MOBILE # (Cell)...

HOME #...

WORK #...

FAX...

EMAIL..

NAME...

ADDRESS..

....

MOBILE # (Cell)...

HOME #...

WORK #...

FAX...

EMAIL..

NAME...

ADDRESS..

....

MOBILE # (Cell)...

HOME #...

WORK #...

FAX...

EMAIL..

NOTES:

NAME..

ADDRESS..

....

MOBILE # (Cell)...

HOME #..

WORK #..

FAX..

EMAIL..

NAME..

ADDRESS..

....

MOBILE # (Cell)...

HOME #..

WORK #..

FAX..

EMAIL..

NAME..

ADDRESS..

....

MOBILE # (Cell)...

HOME #..

WORK #..

FAX..

EMAIL..

<u>**NOTES:**</u>

NAME..
ADDRESS...
....
MOBILE # (Cell)...
HOME #..
WORK #..
FAX...
EMAIL...

NAME..
ADDRESS...
....
MOBILE # (Cell)...
HOME #..
WORK #..
FAX...
EMAIL...

NAME..
ADDRESS...
....
MOBILE # (Cell)...
HOME #..
WORK #..
FAX...
EMAIL...

NOTES:

NAME...

ADDRESS..

....

MOBILE # (Cell)...

HOME #...

WORK #...

FAX...

EMAIL..

NAME...

ADDRESS..

....

MOBILE # (Cell)...

HOME #...

WORK #...

FAX...

EMAIL..

NAME...

ADDRESS..

....

MOBILE # (Cell)...

HOME #...

WORK #...

FAX...

EMAIL..

NOTES:

NAME..

ADDRESS..

....

MOBILE # (Cell)...

HOME #...

WORK #...

FAX...

EMAIL...

NAME..

ADDRESS..

....

MOBILE # (Cell)...

HOME #...

WORK #...

FAX...

EMAIL...

NAME..

ADDRESS..

....

MOBILE # (Cell)...

HOME #...

WORK #...

FAX...

EMAIL...

NOTES:

NAME..
ADDRESS..
....
MOBILE # (Cell)...
HOME #..
WORK #..
FAX...
EMAIL..

NAME..
ADDRESS..
....
MOBILE # (Cell)...
HOME #..
WORK #..
FAX...
EMAIL..

NAME..
ADDRESS..
....
MOBILE # (Cell)...
HOME #..
WORK #..
FAX...
EMAIL..

NOTES:

NAME..

ADDRESS..

....

MOBILE # (Cell)...

HOME #...

WORK #...

FAX..

EMAIL...

NAME..

ADDRESS..

....

MOBILE # (Cell)...

HOME #...

WORK #...

FAX..

EMAIL...

NAME..

ADDRESS..

....

MOBILE # (Cell)...

HOME #...

WORK #...

FAX..

EMAIL...

NOTES:

NAME...

ADDRESS...

....

MOBILE # (Cell)...

HOME #...

WORK #...

FAX..

EMAIL...

NAME...

ADDRESS...

....

MOBILE # (Cell)...

HOME #...

WORK #...

FAX..

EMAIL...

NAME...

ADDRESS...

....

MOBILE # (Cell)...

HOME #...

WORK #...

FAX..

EMAIL...

NOTES:

NAME...

ADDRESS...

....

MOBILE # (Cell)...

HOME #...

WORK #...

FAX...

EMAIL..

NAME...

ADDRESS...

....

MOBILE # (Cell)...

HOME #...

WORK #...

FAX...

EMAIL..

NAME...

ADDRESS...

....

MOBILE # (Cell)...

HOME #...

WORK #...

FAX...

EMAIL..

NOTES:

NAME..

ADDRESS..

....

MOBILE # (Cell)..

HOME #...

WORK #...

FAX..

EMAIL...

NAME..

ADDRESS..

....

MOBILE # (Cell)..

HOME #...

WORK #...

FAX..

EMAIL...

NAME..

ADDRESS..

....

MOBILE # (Cell)..

HOME #...

WORK #...

FAX..

EMAIL...

NOTES:

NAME..
ADDRESS..
....
MOBILE # (Cell)...
HOME #...
WORK #...
FAX..
EMAIL...

NAME..
ADDRESS..
....
MOBILE # (Cell)...
HOME #...
WORK #...
FAX..
EMAIL...

NAME..
ADDRESS..
....
MOBILE # (Cell)...
HOME #...
WORK #...
FAX..
EMAIL...

NOTES:

NAME...
ADDRESS..
....
MOBILE # (Cell)..
HOME #...
WORK #..
FAX...
EMAIL...

NAME...
ADDRESS..
....
MOBILE # (Cell)..
HOME #...
WORK #..
FAX...
EMAIL...

NAME...
ADDRESS..
....
MOBILE # (Cell)..
HOME #...
WORK #..
FAX...
EMAIL...

NOTES:

NAME...

ADDRESS...

....

MOBILE # (Cell)...

HOME #...

WORK #...

FAX...

EMAIL..

NAME...

ADDRESS...

....

MOBILE # (Cell)...

HOME #...

WORK #...

FAX...

EMAIL..

NAME...

ADDRESS...

....

MOBILE # (Cell)...

HOME #...

WORK #...

FAX...

EMAIL..

NOTES:

NAME..

ADDRESS...

....

MOBILE # (Cell)...

HOME #...

WORK #...

FAX..

EMAIL..

NAME..

ADDRESS...

....

MOBILE # (Cell)...

HOME #...

WORK #...

FAX..

EMAIL..

NAME..

ADDRESS...

....

MOBILE # (Cell)...

HOME #...

WORK #...

FAX..

EMAIL..

NOTES:

NAME..
ADDRESS..
....
MOBILE # (Cell)...
HOME #...
WORK #...
FAX..
EMAIL..

NAME..
ADDRESS..
....
MOBILE # (Cell)...
HOME #...
WORK #...
FAX..
EMAIL..

NAME..
ADDRESS..
....
MOBILE # (Cell)...
HOME #...
WORK #...
FAX..
EMAIL..

NOTES:

NAME...
ADDRESS...
....
MOBILE # (Cell)...
HOME #...
WORK #...
FAX...
EMAIL...

NAME...
ADDRESS...
....
MOBILE # (Cell)...
HOME #...
WORK #...
FAX...
EMAIL...

NAME...
ADDRESS...
....
MOBILE # (Cell)...
HOME #...
WORK #...
FAX...
EMAIL...

NOTES:

NAME...
ADDRESS...
....
MOBILE # (Cell)..
HOME #..
WORK #...
FAX...
EMAIL..

NAME...
ADDRESS...
....
MOBILE # (Cell)..
HOME #..
WORK #...
FAX...
EMAIL..

NAME...
ADDRESS...
....
MOBILE # (Cell)..
HOME #..
WORK #...
FAX...
EMAIL..

NOTES:

NAME...

ADDRESS...

....

MOBILE # (Cell)..

HOME #...

WORK #..

FAX..

EMAIL...

NAME...

ADDRESS...

....

MOBILE # (Cell)..

HOME #...

WORK #..

FAX..

EMAIL...

NAME...

ADDRESS...

....

MOBILE # (Cell)..

HOME #...

WORK #..

FAX..

EMAIL...

NOTES:

NAME..

ADDRESS..

....

MOBILE # (Cell)..

HOME #...

WORK #...

FAX...

EMAIL..

NAME..

ADDRESS..

....

MOBILE # (Cell)..

HOME #...

WORK #...

FAX ....

EMAIL..

NAME..

ADDRESS..

....

MOBILE # (Cell)..

HOME #...

WORK #...

FAX...

EMAIL..

NOTES:

NAME..

ADDRESS..

....

MOBILE # (Cell)..

HOME #...

WORK #...

FAX...

EMAIL..

NAME..

ADDRESS..

....

MOBILE # (Cell)..

HOME #...

WORK #...

FAX...

EMAIL..

NAME..

ADDRESS..

....

MOBILE # (Cell)..

HOME #...

WORK #...

FAX...

EMAIL..

NOTES:

NAME...

ADDRESS..

....

MOBILE # (Cell)..

HOME #...

WORK #...

FAX..

EMAIL..

NAME...

ADDRESS..

....

MOBILE # (Cell)..

HOME #...

WORK #...

FAX..

EMAIL..

NAME...

ADDRESS..

....

MOBILE # (Cell)..

HOME #...

WORK #...

FAX..

EMAIL..

NOTES:

NAME..

ADDRESS..

....

MOBILE # (Cell)..

HOME #..

WORK #..

FAX..

EMAIL..

NAME..

ADDRESS..

....

MOBILE # (Cell)..

HOME #..

WORK #..

FAX..

EMAIL..

NAME..

ADDRESS..

....

MOBILE # (Cell)..

HOME #..

WORK #..

FAX..

EMAIL..

NOTES:

NAME..

ADDRESS..

....

MOBILE # (Cell)...

HOME #..

WORK #..

FAX..

EMAIL...

NAME..

ADDRESS..

....

MOBILE # (Cell)...

HOME #..

WORK #..

FAX..

EMAIL...

NAME..

ADDRESS..

....

MOBILE # (Cell)...

HOME #..

WORK #..

FAX..

EMAIL...

NOTES:

www.ingramcontent.com/pod-product-compliance
Lightning Source LLC
Chambersburg PA
CBHW060513220326
41598CB00025B/3641